# Journey into the skin

## Co-Exist with psoriasis

# Giovanni Salierno

# Journey into
# the skin

## Co-Exist with psoriasis

*Journey into the skin  - Giovanni Salierno*

Copyright © 2021 Giovanni Salierno


ISBN: 9798718741018

Names and places of the stories have been modified in order to protect the privacy of the interviewees. Any similarity to actual people, living or dead, places or events is purely coincidental.

Cover picture by Roberto Della Noce
Translated by Alessia Palmers

© I Italian edition: September 2020
© I English edition: April 2021

# From the same author:

- *La deformazione del sé nello sguardo dell'altro: Con-Vivere con la psoriasi*

- *Viaggio nella pelle: Con-Vivere con la psoriasi*

Translated in english:
- *Journey into the skin: Co-Exist with psoriasis*

- *L'illusione di Eco … l'inganno di Narciso*

- *L'abbraccio di Gipsy*

- *L'anima di Gipsy*

- *Le anime raccontano Gipsy*

- *Il Tango di Gispy*

# Summary

*"He stares again, again at the twin stars that are his eyes; at his fair hair, which can compare with Bacchus' or with Apollo's; at his beardless cheeks and at his ivory neck, his splendid mouth, the pink blush on a face as white as snow...*

*How many futile kisses did he waste on the deceptive pool! ...*

*He knows not what he sees, but what he sees invites him..."*

*Ovid (Metamorphoses III, 420 et seq.)*

# On Beauty

And a poet said, Speak to us of Beauty.

And he answered: Where shall you seek beauty, and how shall you find her unless she herself be your way and your guide? And how shall you speak of her except she be the weaver of your speech?

The aggrieved and the injured say, "Beauty is kind and gentle. Like a young mother half-shy of her own glory she walks among us."

And the passionate say, "Nay, beauty is a thing of might and dread. Like the tempest she shakes the earth beneath us and the sky above us."

The tired and the weary say, "Beauty is of soft whisperings. She speaks in our spirit. Her voice yields to our silences like a faint light that quivers in fear of the shadow." But the restless say, "We have heard her shouting among the mountains. And with her cries came the sound of hoofs, and the beating of wings and the roaring of lions."

At night the watchmen of the city say, "Beauty shall rise with the dawn from the east." And at noontide the toilers and the way-farers say, "We have seen her leaning over the earth from the windows of the sunset."

In winter say the snow-bound, "She shall come with the spring leaping upon the hills."

And in the summer heat the reapers say,

"We have seen her dancing with the autumn leaves, and we saw a drift of snow in her hair." All these things have you said of beauty. Yet in truth you spoke not of her but of needs unsatisfied.

And beauty is not a need but an ecstasy.

It is not a mouth thirsting nor an empty hand stretched forth. But rather a heart enflamed and a soul enchanted.

It is not the image you would see nor the song you would hear, but rather an image you see though you close your eyes and a song you hear though you shut your ears.

It is not the sap within the furrowed bark, nor a wing attached to a claw.

But rather a garden forever in bloom anda flock of angels forever in flight.

People of Orphalese, beauty is life when life unveils her holy face.

But you are life and you are the veil.

Beauty is eternity gazing at itself in a mirror.

But you are eternity and you are the mirror.

*"The Prophet" Kahlil Gibran*

# Preface

My Journey into the skin has lasted for over twenty years. A car accident marked the beginning of this disease.

Many changes in lifestyle and the will to understand this condition led me to study psychology and to become a psychologist today.

Psoriasis affects not only the body, but also the psyche.

Today self-esteem is put to the test. Be imperfect is critical in a society where appearance is what matters the most.

This disease forces people to not be themselves anymore, it leads them to isolate themselves in order not to be marginalized by others who see them as "monsters".

While reading this book psoriasis will not disappear from the body, but maybe we can learn to cope whit it.

# Introduction

In Ovid's story, probably based on the version of Phartenius, but modified, Echo is a mountain nymph, she falls in love with a vain young man named Narcissus son of Cephissus, a river god, and the nymph Liriope.
Cephissus surrounded Liriope with his rivers, and seduced her, so she gave birth to an extremely handsome child.

Worried for the future of the child, Liriope consulted the seer Tiresias, who predicted that Narcissus would live a long life only "if he never discovered himself".

When Narcissus turned sixteen, he was young and so handsome that everyone in the city, man or woman, young or old, fell in love with him. But he, proudly, rejected them all.

One day, while the young man was hunting deer, the nymph Echo stealthily followed him into the woods, because she wanted to talk to him.

She was incapable of talking first, she was forced to always repeat the last words that were said to her.

She was forced to do so because she had been punished by Juno when, with long stories, she distracted her allowing the other nymphs, Jupiter's lovers, to hide. Narcissus heard the footsteps and shouted "Who's there?", Echo repeated "who's there?" and so they went on until the nymph revealed her identity and ran to hug the boy.

But he stepped away and told her to leave him alone.

Echo, with a broken heart, spent the rest of her life in lonely glens, crying for her unreciprocated love, until nothing but her voice was left of her.

Nemesis, listening to these cries decided to punish the cruel Narcissus.

One day the young man, while in the woods, came across a deep pond and got closer to it to drink.

As soon as he saw, for the first time in his life his reflection, he fell madly in love with the boy who was staring back at him, without realizing it was his own reflection.

Only after a while he noticed that it was his own reflection and, realizing that that love could never be achieved, he let himself die.

The prophecy of Tiresias was fulfilled. When the Naiads and the Dryad wanted to take his body and place it on the funeral pyre, they found a flower in his place, who was given the name Narcissus.

Story goes that when Narcissus crossed the Styx, the river of the dead, to enter the underworld, he looked at the muddy waters of the river hoping to see his reflection once again.[1]

Beauty shines more in the heart of those who aspire to it, that in the eyes of those who see it.[2]

We cannot see ourselves as beautiful when the face that we see reflected in the mirror is disfigured by a skin disease such as psoriasis. But, if we look for comfort in the

---

[1] There are different versions of the myth of Narcissus, this is the roman one narrated by Ovid in book III of his Metamorphoses.
[2] Kahlil Gibran, "The Prophet", on beauty.

eyes of others, the reflection can come back even more monstrous than before. Feeling beautiful is probably more important now that in the past, because beauty, in modern society, is almost a social obligation.

Being beautiful means belonging to society, be accepted, be desired and requested. These are the factors that build confidence and social identity in each person.

Then what can we say about a disease such as psoriasis, that affects our image, the "beauty" of the body and sometimes of the face?

The classical myth of Narcissus symbolizes the role of self-reflection, but in order to be accepted, it is fundamental that the first visual impact with the other is positive.

Beauty costs Narcissus his life, to the person with psoriasis the disease brings "despair".

Those who have a face disfigured by psoriasis can never look good.

A good-looking person is someone who is pleasing to the eye, which is impossible for people with psoriasis, where the skin is disfigured by spots or scabs.

If people with psoriasis see their reflection in the water do not see someone to fall in love with, but the image of a monster to run away from.

That means running away from ourselves, but mostly from whom, looking at us, makes us feel unpleasant.

# Chapter I: Psoriasis

## *1.1 Then and now*

Psoriasis affects about 100 million people around the world, it increases with age and differs from one population to another; in Italy it affects about two million and a half people. In the west world about 3-4% of the population has it.[3]

This is one of the oldest skin diseases. In fact, some representations can be found in the Egyptian papyri and is clearly recognizable in some pages of the bible.[4]

A detailed description of this disease can be found in Hippocratic Corpus published

---

[3] ADIPSO, http://www.adipso.org.

[4] Leviticus, "Book of Job". The Bible talks about a skin disease that affected Job's skin and of Hezekiah's skin lesion, cured with fig poultices.

in Alessandria about a century after the death of Hippocrates (430-377 B.C.) and later in the work of Celso of 35-40 A.C.[5]

In ancient times, in the Middle Ages and until the middle of the last century it was mistaken for a type of leprosy, not mutilating and not contagious.

Called, in its chronic and stable form; "lepra graecorum"; "psora leprosa" in its active or unstable form, polycyclic and confluent. Until the beginning of the 19th century the term "lepra" was used to describe the disease.[6]

It was only towards the end of this century that it was proved that the two forms mentioned were both the same disease and that it had nothing to do with leprosy and, therefore, the people affected did not have to be isolated from society, because their disease was not contagious.[7]

---

[5] In the 5th century B.C. Hippocrates gives us a detailed description of the psoriatic lesions and calls this disease "Psora".

[6] Willam, R, "On cutaneous diseases". Volumen I. Londres, 1808.

[7] Hebra F., "Atlas der Hautkrankheiten". Vienna, 1856-1876.

The disease appears for the first time around the age of thirty-nine (59% of the affected), the peak is between the age of twenty and thirty-nine.[8]

Psoriasis is an inflammatory disease of the skin, it is hereditary, caused by several factors. So, it is not only hereditary, but it can also be caused by stress.

It is the stress that, in addition to causing the disease, can also make it worse. On the body surface, due to inflammation of the skin, appear red spots and plaques.

This is due to an abnormal increase in the production of the outermost layer of the epidermis.

The renewal of the outer layer of the skin usually occurs every twenty-eight days, while in a person with psoriasis it happens seven times faster.

As a result, cells that are not fully mature build up on the surface of the skin.

---

[8] Naldi L. et al. Study design and preliminary results from the pilot phase of the Praktis study: self-reported diagnoses of selected skin disease in a representative sample of the Italian population, dermatology, 208: 38-42, 2004.

There are different types of psoriasis, with different symptoms.

There is still no complete and common classification. However, usually the different types of psoriasis are identified as; plague psoriasis, guttate psoriasis, inverse psoriasis, pustular psoriasis, erythrodermic psoriasis, desquamative psoriasis andarthropathic psoriasis.

As it is the case for most physical diseases for which there is a chromosomal predisposition, the alleged vulnerability can cause the development of a pathology when the patient is subjected to stress.[9]

Although predisposition to psoriasis is genetic, external factors such as stress, can directly affect the spread of skin lesions. This physical disease does not have to be seen only from the medical point of view, but the social and psychological factors must be considered too.

Psoriasis can have devastating effects on the quality of life and social relations. It can

---

[9] Zubin, J., & Spring, B. (1977). "Vulnerability new view of schizophrenia". Journal of Abnormal Psychology, 86, 103-126.

also compromise the social life of the person affected.

It cannot really be considered a skin disease, because the disease itself and its worsening are all caused by multiple factors, including some phyco-social factors.

In modern society, especially in the west society, physical appearance and external beauty are extremely important.

Beauty has always been a criterion for comparison, but today, due to mass-media, it is even more important.

Beauty increases power and social recognition.

It is not only important in everyday life, in order to be accepted by others and by the partner, but also to find a job.[10]

Who does not live up to the beauty stereotypes is pushed aside through stigmatization processes.[11]

---

[10] Waters J. (1985), "Cosmetics and the job market". In J. Graham, A. Klingman (eds.), "The Psychology of cosmetics treatments", New York, Praeger.
[11] Goffman E., "Stigma", 1963, Italian translation, Veron, Ombre corte, 2003

Who does not live up to the beauty stereotypes is pushed aside through stigmatization processes.

People with psoriasis feel stigmatized and rejected by others and it can affect their job, it can lead to alcohol abuse and to the need for psychiatric care.

The 19% of people with psoriasis claimed that they have experienced rejection in the workplace, at school, at the hair salon, at the gym and in other public places.[12]

These rejections or the feeling of repulsion from others lead to serious problems of adaptation at work and to emotional problems.

Sometimes they can also lead to alcoholism and excessive use of cigarettes.

The increased use of alcohol in patients with psoriasis is more a socio psychological consequence of the disease than a major determining cause.[13]

---

[12] Ginzburg IH, Link Bg. (1993) "Psychosocial consequences of rejection and stigma feelings in psoriasis patient". Int Dermatology; 32: 587-91.

[13] Naldi L., Parazzini F, Brevi A, et al. "Family history, smoking habits, alcohol consumption and risk of psoriasis". Br J Dermatology 1992; 127: 212-217.

---

Alcohol consumption is higher in men with chronic psoriasis than in men without it.[14]

However, while at the beginning it does not appear to be higher than that of healthy people, it increases progressively with the severity and probably also with the duration of the disease.

In patients with psoriasis there is a clear prevalence of smokers, mostly women.[15]

But it is difficult to establish if smoke can cause the disease or if it is a consequence, as for alcohol.

---

[14] The control group consists of people who, during an experiment, are kept under the same conditions as those examined. However, they are not subjected to the treatment studied.

[15] Braathen LR, Botten G, Bjerkedal T. Psoriatics in Norway. Acta Derm Venereol 1989; 142(Suppl): 9-12. 16 Montagu A., Touching, The Human Significance of the Skin, Published by Columbia University Press/NY in 1971. A Book Review by Bobby Matherne 2006. 17 Lazarus R.S. e Folkman S., Stress, appraisal and coping, New York, Springer, 1984.

## 1.2 *The impact of psoriasis: wellbeing and coping*

The skin is the most important sense organ, since it is strictly related not only to the physical, but also to the behavioral development of the individual.
The skin shows internal problems of the body that cannot be expressed otherwise.[16]

Situations that cause a deep change in the life of the individual are very stressful. Stress is a set of processes involving interactions between the individual and the environment.

People feel stressed when there is a discrepancy between a situation and the abilities that the person has in order to face it.[17]

---

[16] Montagu A., Touching, "The Human Significance of the Skin", Published by Columbia University Press/ NY in 1971. A Book Review by Bobby Matherne 2006.
[17] Lazarus R.S. and Folkman S., "Stress, appraisal

---

Usually, before the disease, there is one or more stressful situations, even though the patient does not always identify them.

Even the loss of someone or something, the loss of the old for the new, can be stressful.

In fact, the disease can manifest itself even after positive events, such as marriage, a moment of deep change.

Not only specific stressful situations, but also the stress caused by everyday life can damage the person's health.[18]

Stressful are those events that change the situation and the life of the individual, demanding a considerable effort of adaptation.

Patients with this skin disease face the world, with its challenges, protecting themselves with some sort of armor. Psychological and somatic factors always interact and influence each other, creating a

---

and coping", New York, Springer, 1984.
[18] Picardi A, Pasquini P, Abeni D, Fassone G., Mazzotti E, Fava GA. Psychosomatic assessment of skin diseases in clinical practice. Psychotherapy and Psychosomatics, 2005, 74:315-22.

physical armor on the skin due to skin thickening.

The characteristics of patients with psoriasis are: emotional inhibition, anger management, severe anxiety, forced phantasmatic life and alexithymia.

The kind of psychological defenses that people with psoriasis use in order to deal with their life experiences are neurotic; they avoid, deny, repress and isolate their feelings.

The psychological discomfort is denied because patients are more attached to their physical symptoms.

Since psoriasis is a disease that affects not only health, but also the quality of life, different indexes have been developed in order to study this impact. Among the major indexes that measures the physical impact, there is the P.A.S.I. (Psoriasis Area and Severity Index).

While the DLQI is used to measure the impact on the quality of life.[19]

---

[19] Finlay AY, Khan GK. Dermatology Life Quality Index (DLQI): a simple practical measure for routine clinical use. Clin Exp Dermatology, 1994; 19:210-216.

P.A.S.I. is an index that gives a score to the severity of psoriasis.

When the index is used the damaged area is taken into consideration,[20] which means how much skin is affected by the disease.

In other words, the inflammation, the redness of the area, are analyzed; it also analyzes how much higher this damaged skin part is compared to the skin that surrounds it.

This is done in order to understand the infiltration of the disease.

Lastly the desquamation is analyzed, that means how many scales have fallen from this area or how many silver-white scales has the area.

---

[20] To measure how invalidating the disease is, severity indexes are used to analyze the skin area. The body is divided into four sections; head which represents 10% of the skin, arms which are 20%, trunk which is 30% and legs which are 40%. The percent of skin affected in each area is associated with a score that goes from zero (no involvement) to six (over 90% of involvement).
The severity is measured by taking into consideration four different parameters: itchiness, erythema, desquamation and thickness.

The main criticism made to the use of P.A.S.I is that there is no patient's point of view, since the severity of the disease is measured by the doctor, without the patient's opinion.[21]

Psoriasis has a specific impact on the quality of life which does not have to be measured by the severity of the disease on the skin, but by the assessment of psychological stress, mistrust in relations with others and society due to phenomena of stigmatization which can negatively affect work or school productivity.[22]

The psycho-social factors vary from disease to disease, from person to person. They can even change in the same person from one episode to another.

In fact, in some cases it can have a greater impact on life a slight, barely visible desquamation, than a noticeable dermatitis.[23]

---

[21] McHenry PM, Doherty VR. "Psoriasis: an audit of patients' views on the disease and its treatment." Br J Dermatology 1992 127: 13-7.

[22] Rapp SR, Feldman SR. Exum ML et al. "Psoriasis causes as much disability as other major medical disease". J Am Acad Dermatology 1999; 41: 401-407.

[23] LipowskiZj, "Psychosomatic medicine in the

It can happen sometimes that with psoriasis reduced to 80%, so with little, almost invisible signs, the doctor may consider it as a success, while the patient can still have the same or even worse problems of stigma, shame, fear and difficulty in the relationship with the other.[24]

The traditional measurement of the P.A.S.I. measure the severity of the disease analyzing, for example, the percentage of skin surface affected or the size of the scales, but it does not consider the consequences that the disease may have on the person.

However, in recent years, the concept of quality of life (QOL) has developed considerably, based on physical, social and psychological factors.[25]

---

seventies: an overview." Am J Psychiatry 1977: 134: 233-234.

[24] Abeni D., Picardi A., Pasquini P., Melchi CF., Chern MM (2002) "Further evidence of the validity and reliability of the Skindex-29: an italian Study on 2.242 dermatological outpatients". Dermatology 204:43-9.

[25] Anderson RT, Rajagopalan R. (1997). "Development and validation of a quality of life instruments for cutaneous diseases". J Am Acad

Psoriasis does not only negatively affects the quality of life of those affected, but it also affects the life of their families.

In fact, the duration of the treatment, the unwillingness to live alone or mostly at home, closed inside a house, avoiding public places, sport activities, beaches, the sea. These can all have an influence on how relatives spend their free time.[26]

In order to establish how much a disease negatively affects the mood of the patient, different tests, such as DLQI, have been developed.[27]

---

Fermato; 37: 41-50.

[26] Ramsay B. O'Reagan M. "A survey of the social and psychological effects of psoriasis". 1988: 195-201.

[27] The Skindex-29, the skindex-17 and the SF-36. The skindex-29 is a self-administered questionnaire that asses the importance of symptoms, social function and emotional state.
This questionnaire has very good psychometric properties and it is easy to administer. It has thirty questions, so it only takes five minutes to complete. It includes ten parameters related to the emotional sphere: seven concerning the symptoms of the patient and twelve to analyze the functional aspects. The Skindex-17 is a reduction and refinement of the Skindex-29 developed by the team of the I.D.I.

DLQI measures how much psoriasis influences the life of the person affected.

It is s a questionnaire that takes into consideration the skin problems and their impact on the patient's life over the last seven days.[28]

Other indexes and scales take into consideration the area of the body affected by psoriasis or the disability it entails, or the quality of life or the psychophysical condition of the patient. The purpose is always to try to measure if, how and how

---

in collaboration with Mary-Margaret Chern and Tamar Nijsten.

The SF-36 has been developed since the 1980s in the united states of America. It is a multidimensional questionnaire with thirty-six questions that allow to create eight different scales. Patients, on average, take about ten minutes to complete it.

The thirty-six questions refer to eight domains of health: physical functioning, role limitations due to physical health problems, role limitations due to emotional problems, body pain, general health perception, vitality, social functioning, mental health and changes in health status.

[28] Finlay AY, Coles EC. "The effect of severe psoriasis on the quality of life of 369 patients". Br J Dermatology 1995; 132: 236-244.

---

much the therapeutic intervention has influenced the disease, but not how the person can live in society.

In order to measure the QOL of patients with psoriasis, several factors are taken into account; symptoms, work or school, the simple daily activities, sexual activity, drinking or smoking, suicidal thoughts, family and stigmatization.

Usually, the physical symptoms that patients with psoriasis have are: pain, itching, burning and dry skin.

In a study based on one hundred and four patients, 30% of them have described the itching as the worst symptom.[29]

The severity of the physical symptoms is to be considered according to the opinions of patients and their physical conditions (25%).[30]

Psoriasis influences even the easiest daily activities. It can influence the haircut, the color and style of clothes, participation in

---

[29] Ramsay B. O' Reagan M. "A survey of the social and psychological effects of psoriasis." 1988: 195-201

[30] McHenry PM, Doherty VR. "Psoriasis: an audit of patients' views on the disease and its treatment." Br J Dermatology 1992 127: 13-7.

social activities such as sports or simple manual activities which affect the skin by sweating or bleeding.

They also prevent people from going to the pool or to the beach, places avoided by all people with psoriasis both in its severe or less severe form.

Even though sexual responsiveness has not been related to the severity of the disease or with its location in genital areas, it was found that many patients, especially women, find it difficult to start sexual relationships.[31]

In addition, about 10% of patients with psoriasis, also have suicidal thoughts, this further emphasizes the mind-body connection.

Usually, suicidal thoughts are more common in patients with high depressive scores and in those who think they have a severe form of psoriasis.[32]

---

[31] Van Dorssen IE, Boom BW, Hengeveld MW. "Experience of sexuality in patients with psoriasis and constitutional eczema. Ned Tijdschr Geneeskd" 1992; 136: 2175-8.

[32] Cotterill J.A. Cunliffe WJ. "Suicide in dermatological patients." Br J Dermatology 1997; 137: 246-250.

As we have already seen, the disease does not only affect the daily life of the people affected and their social functioning, but it also compromises the quality of life of their families.

Friends and especially relatives are involved in the daily life of people with psoriasis.

The treatment duration, the frequent unwillingness to leave the house and to go to different public places, can also influence the family's free time, since in some cases, especially the most severe, relative are morally, physically and financially involved.[33]

---

[33] Ramsay B. O' Reagan M. "A survey of the social and psychological effects of psoriasis". 1988: 195-201.

## *1.3 Beauty and stigma*

Beauty has a key role in a world where friends, partners and coworkers relate to us and with the same level of content of communication and ability to establish new relationships, good looking and healthy people are more persuasive than those who are ugly and sick.

Many researches show how beauty plays an important role when choosing the partner and in the development of intimate personal relationships.

At the beginning of a relationship with an attractive person, both men and women tend to lie, changing their characteristics for the better.

Such as, for example, personality traits, income, personal success, job skills and intelligence.[34]

---

[34] Rowatt W. C., Cunningham M. R., Druen P. B., 1999, Lying to get a date: The effect official physical attractiveness on the willingness to deceive prospective dating partners, "Journal of Social and

Even on a judicial level good looking people are judged less guilty than those who are not attractive and their behavior, even if wrong, is often justified by "external causes" such as "circumstances" rather than directly associated with the will.

In order to understand how important attractiveness and beauty are in modern society, we need to think about those cases in which it turns out to be deficient.

For example, in cases of skin diseases such as psoriasis.

Skin diseases and lesions, that compromise the exteriority of the body, may affect negatively social relationships. They can affect the psychological balance of the people affected and there is, at times, the necessity for psychological therapies. Attractiveness is important even when looking for a job. In fact, the success of people, such as actors and models may depend more on beauty than skills.

Even when hiring, especially for a job that requires contact with the public, salespeople, flight attendant, public relations careers, beauty is very important.

Personal Relationships" 16, 209-223.

Considering that people that are more attractive tend to have greater social skills and extroversion.[35]

It has also been proved that good looking people are more likely to find a job and have more important jobs.

Usually for specific jobs, good looking people are preferred.

Research on the possibility to find a job based on physical beauty did not have the same results for males and females. For managerial positions and positions of responsibility beauty is an advantage for men, but not for women.

With attractive people prejudices on the ability of men and women to do certain jobs are more noticeable (beautiful women are considered more suitable for jobs considered as women's careers than women who are less attractive).

In addition, If a woman gets promoted quickly, it is usually associated more with

---

[35] Dipboye R., Arvey R. Terpstra D., 1977, "Sex and physical attractiveness of raters and applicants as determinants of résumé evaluations", Journal of Applied Psychology, 62, 288-294.

beauty than skills and this is caused by social prejudices.[36]

One of the reasons why beauty influences everyday psychology is because it is associated with different positive characteristics that are actually independent. Psychologists call this phenomenon "halo effect"; a certain feature, such as the attractiveness of a person, as a halo, influences his or her other features and our impression turns out to be distorted.

One of the reasons why beauty influences everyday psychology is because it is associated with different positive characteristics that are actually independent. Psychologists call this phenomenon "halo effect"; a certain feature, such as the attractiveness of a person, as a halo, influences his or her other features and our impression turns out to be distorted.[37]

---

[36] Waters J. (1985), "Cosmetics and the job market." In J. Graham, A. Kligman (eds.), The Psychology of cosmetics treatments, New York, Praeger.

[37] Based on ninety-three studies who have tried to understand if attractive and unattractive people differed in some personality traits, the overall analysis has revealed a total lack of relation between

Physical beauty on the other hand, has other kind of effects; for example, it can encourage more interpersonal contact and it can reduce social anxiety.[38]

So, beauty is not only important in our society, but being good looking also improves one's self-esteem and confidence. This does not happen in people with psoriasis that, due to the disease, feel ugly.

Who does not conform to beauty stereotypes is marginalized through different processes and phenomena, as can happen with stigmatization.

Through the social phenomenon of stigmatization, a member (or a group) of the community is associated with a negative connotation and seen as inferior. There are four stages that lead to social stigma.[39]

In the first stage biological, psychological or social differences are selected. They can be used to discriminate others.

---

physical attractiveness and qualities such as intelligence, dominance or other.

[38] Feingold A., (1992), Good-looking people are not we think, "Psychological Bullettin" 21, 304-341.

[39] Goffman E., "Stigma", 1963, italian translation, Verona, Ombre corte, 2003.

---

In the second stage negative stereotypes are attributed to these artificial categories.

In the third stage a distinction is made between stigmatized and not stigmatized people. Finally, with the fourth stage there is the actual loss of status for the stigmatized individual.

Most stigmatized people try to rebel against this unfair process.

The rejection of stigma occurs through three main ways; by hiding the clues on which the social stigma is based, using techniques of neutralization to justify the deviance, especially in the case of social deviance and ultimately, trying to organize a support group with other people who suffer from the same stigma.

All three methods are used by patients with psoriasis. In fact, these people in order to hide their disease, cover themselves with hairs, pants and shirts with long sleeves, even during the summer.

While women let their hair grow, men hide their face with bears too.

Usually, people with a severe form of psoriasis shut themselves away.

They do not leave the house, end all contact with the outside world. In doing so, they do not give others the chance to watch and judge.

Since the culture in which we live in demands a nice appearance, there is a psycho-social stigma that sometimes becomes even more debilitating than the symptom itself.

Being unattractive is not only not positive, but it can even become negative.

The social identity of a person is linked to the awareness of belonging to specific social groups and to the emotional meaning that comes from such belonging.

The social world is based on a categorization that is used to organize the context.

Such categorization represents an orientation system that creates and defines the place of an individual in society.

We can say that for the person affected by psoriasis the disease becomes a form of social identity.

Each person belongs to a system that is divided into categories.

The main consequence of belonging to a group is that it leads people to try to stay in it and also to try to join other groups, if these can reinforce the positive aspects of their social identity.[40]

In our case the disease would categorize people by putting them into a group with characteristics such as stigma and rejection.

---

[40] Michael Billig, Henri Tajfel. "Social categorization and similarity in intergroup behavior", 1972.

# Chapter II: The self through skin

## *2.1 Skin: container creator of bonds and protective shield*

Skin, the largest organ of the human body, is not only important from a biological point of view, but also from a psychological one.

The surface of the human body is the place were perceptions from the outside and the inside can occur at the same time.

This is fundamental in the creation of the ego and in its differentiation from the id.[41]

At the beginning of existence be caressed, hold, calmed by skin contact helps the child to create an image of the body and

---

[41] Freud S., "L'io e l'Es", 1922, OSF, vol. 9, Bollati Boringhieri, Torino.

of a healthy body ego. It increases the self-love and, at the same time, encourages the development of objective love,  rengthening the bonds between mother and son.[42]

Skin is an important organ in the development of human behavior. Caresses, cuddles, hugs, in early childhood play an important role in the further development of the individual.

The child needs to understand, through touch, what intimacy, proximity, distance and separation mean.[43]

Through perception people acknowledge that they are separated from the outside world.

After the first year of life appear visual images called "fantasies about the body". That, along with the progressive consolidation of the boundaries of the Self, will create in the mind, the body image and a first image of the self. So, the body image is the mental representation of the bodily self.[44]

---

[42] Anna Freud, 1936. L'io e i meccanismi di difesa, Florence, G.Martinelli, 1967.

[43] Montagu A., 1971, "Touching. the human significance of the skin."

The body as the place of the psyche is delimited by skin. Children through the experience of the body surface, can represent themselves as an ego capable of protecting the psychic contents.

The skin has different functions; it breaths and perspire, secretes and remove, keeps the tone, stimulates breathing, circulation, digestion, excretion and reproduction.[45]

The child's skin is subjected to attentive maternal care.

There is a wide range of contacts with the child's skin; caresses, rubbing, recurrent small pinches, contacts by air (when breathing on the face or body of the child), kisses.

Body contact has a containment function, a good enough mother for the child will touch him, give him body warmth, movements and tranquility according to the necessities of the child.[46]

---

[44] 44 Gaddini E., "Il Sé in psicoanalisi", 1982, Milano, Cortina.

[45] 45 Anzieu D.,1985, "L'io pelle", Roma, Borla, 1994

[46] D. 1960, Sviluppo affettivo e ambiente, Armando Editore, 1983.

---

The skin delimits people, identifying them. Is the organ that is visibly in contact with others.

It is a part that touches and is touched, "knowing" and "diversifying" at the same time itself and the outside world. Children, for example, through tactile experiences learn to know and to distinguish their body from others.[47]

So, skin is a limit, protection, defense, knowledge and communication, so much so that it can change its color revealing one's emotions and feelings to others.[48]

But, when, for any reason, a person denies this communication, from the psychological point of view, maybe he doesn't want to become aware of his emotions or feelings that are annoying, from a psychosomatic point of view, his skin shows this inner drama.

Rage, for example, experienced but not openly manifested, can manifest itself on the skin through eczematous reactions. Redness and stinging become some sort of

---

[47] Anzieu D. "L'io pelle", Ed. Borla, 1987
[48] Scuola di medicina psicosomatica Riza.

somatic manifestation of an inner "fire" that, having no other way of expressing itself, irritates the skin.

So, from a psychosomatic point of view, psoriasis can be seen as an overproduction of scales, to protect itself, creating some sort of armor, and as a very short skin renewal cycle, a failed attempt to "change skin", to be renewed.

This inevitably leads to isolate from others, in order not to be looked at and judged.

Skin is the line that defines and communicates relationships with others. Blushing when embarrassed, for example, calls for both narcissists and sexual libidinal investment. Is the center of well-being and seduction.

It brings pain and pleasure. Skin materializes our nudity, but also our sexual arousal.

With its fragility and vulnerability explains our primal need, which is bigger than that of any other species, and at the same time our ability to adapt and evolve. It separates and connects the different senses separating the inner and the outer world.

When sick, seeing the outside world as something hostile causes the skin to thicken and become like an armor.

But this armor makes people look less attractive, so it makes it difficult for people to look at themselves into the mirror and through the eyes of others.

Narcissus's myth makes us understand the importance of our reflection, the possibility to look at ourselves and admire without fear of seeing, in the reflection, an image that we do not like.

While the red spots on the Narcissus flower may represent uniqueness and beauty, on a person, on the face, the hands, the arms they are a disfigurement.

In fact, having spots on the face makes us fear the possibility of being looked at with curiosity, disgust or disdain.

From the individual point of view is clear how the disease, compromising the appearance, may affect relationships, affectivity, work and may affect the psychological balance of the people affected.

It is clear that skin diseases and lesions, that affect the appearance of the body, may compromise social relationships. They may also affect the psychological balance of people affected that, in some cases, will need psychological therapies.[49]

---

[49] Rowatt W. C., Cunningham M. R., Druen P. B., 1999, Lying to get a date: The effect official physical attractiveness on the willingness to deceive prospective dating partners, "Journal of Social and Personal Relationships" 16, 209-223

## 2.2 *The self in the social process*

The self consists of an exogenous component of social origin the Me, and by another endogenous represented by the I.

The I and the Me are like constitutive elements of the Self, it makes a distinction between the creative I and the conformist Me.

The ideas of a conventional person and those of the people near him, are the same. In these circumstances the person is nothing more than a Me, which adjustments are just superficial.

As opposed to the Me, there is the individual that has a very well-defined personality, that responds to the organized behavior in a significantly different way. In this individual the I is dominant. The I embodies the differentiating and constructive factors of the Self.

The innovative approach that every subject can adopt when facing any kind of social life's problem.

The Me, on the other hand, reflects those information of recognition and disconfirmation that emerge from interpersonal relationships.

People with psoriasis, often remain trapped in the superficial adjustment that the Me carries out, since the I is incapable, with creative answers, of facing the social disconfirmations to which the self is subjected.

The self ends up representing the result of a dialectic tension between two polarities: exogenous and endogenous.

It is the correlation between the I and the Me that constitutes the space for the development of the self.

The self of a person is based on the judgements and signs of recognition or of refusal from others.

Obviously, this only happens in a social contest where there is an interaction between the person and others.

That is, where there are primary and secondary socializations.

So, the self can be considered as a process in which the protagonist is the individual and the society is the "generalized other".

It is procedural and, more precisely, dialectical, where subjective factors are involved, but also the social world, both as representation of the other and as a system of relationships.[50]

The individual can be considered in the double role of actor and character where the self is the result of a social construction that is generated and produced in interactive processes.

As a character the individual produces an image with its ideal and stereotypical positive qualities which must be shown by the presentation.

As an actor, the purpose is to perpetuate a specific definition of the situation and a version of reality.

In our society the character that people portray, and their Self are, in some way, identified. The Self, as character, is usually seen as something that lives in the body of the person who has it.[51]

---

[50] Mead G. H.. "Mind, Self, and Society." Ed. by Charles W. Morris. University of Chicago Press.1934.

[51] Goffman E. "La vita quotidiana come rappresentazione", 1969, ed. Il Mulino, p. 288.

People give a social meaning to the existence of the individual.

There is an intermediate space between the definition of the Self and the interaction defined in the concept of face.

The face of a person is not a part of the body, but rather something that is in the flow of events that takes place during the meeting and that becomes manifest only when the assessment that are expressed in these events are interpreted.[52]

The face marks the meaning that society gives to different forms of expression of the Self.

Once the face is acquired the individual uses it as if it were his or her own property, but this cannot be, since social processes of interaction can revoke it or modify its connotations.

Once a person gets psoriasis, the old "clean" face is replaced by a new face "disfigured" by the disease.

---

[52] Goffman E., Relations in Public: "Microstudies of the Public Order. Relazioni in pubblico. Microstudi sull'ordine pubblico", traslated by Davide Zoletto, collection «Studi», Bompiani,1981.

Starting from the concept of self and face we can focus on the value of social interactions (face to face) and on how they regulate behaviors and symbolic expressions that appear during the relational exchange.[53]

The concept of self cannot grow without a sense of personal control. We refer to people's beliefs of having control over the events of their lives, using the concept of "locus of control".

Especially those who believe that they can determine what happens to them, with their efforts and abilities.

These are called people with an internal locus of control.

Vice versa those who believe that they do not have any control over their life and that believe that the events are determined by external forces such as luck, disease, fate and influence of other important and powerful people. These are called people with an external locus of control.[54]

[53] Goffman E. "Strategic Interaction", in Modelli di interazione, traduzione di Dina Cabrini, collana «Testi e studi», Il Mulino, 1969, pp. 485. L'interazione strategica, traduzione di Dina Cabrini e Vittorio Mortara, collana «Saggi», Il Mulino, 1988, pp. 176.

[54] In psychological sciences, the term Locus of control (internal locus), refers to how people believe that the events of their life are the result of their behavior or actions, or caused by external causes beyond their control. There are two types of locus of control.

Internal: which includes people who believe in their ability to control events. These people attribute their successes or failure to their abilities, will and skills.

External: which includes people who believe that life events, such as rewards or punishments, are not the result of their abilities, but of unpredictable external factors such as chaos, luck or destiny.

The concept of "internal\external locus of control" was first introduced in 1954 by Julian B. Rotter, an American psychologist who developed the theories of Social learning theory and of Locus of control, which have become important frame of reference in psychology, in relation to the study of people's personalities.

# Chapter III: The interview

## *3.1 The narrative interview*

When doing a research in psychology, two main instruments used to gather information are the interview and the questionnaire. Both have specific pros and cons due to the fundamental differences in their structure.

The face-to-face interview is a dyadic interaction between interviewer and interviewee.

The order and form in which questions are asked can be changed.

On the other hand, the questionnaire is a predetermined set of questions, that cannot be changed.

In the questionnaire the answers given by each person can be compared with the answers of others who completed it.

Given the differences in their structures, we can choose to use an instrument instead of the other depending on the purposes of the research.

We need to take into consideration the kind of information that we want to look for and the amount of knowledge that the researcher has on the subject. The interview can identify the reasons for the behavior, the connections between behaviors and beliefs of an individual. The questionnaire allows to observe the most superficial information such as the attitude of the person.

However, it is unsuitable for exploratory research, since the person has to answer a predetermined set of questions.

To those who fill it in, the questionnaire may also appear as an artificial situation, making them feel the unpleasant impression of being examined.

Questionnaires, such as the P.A.S.I., the Skindex-29 and the Skindex-17, give the possibility of having a group of data, classifiable in categories of belonging, where the definition of the type of answer is already given. The questionnaire could also be made starting from the interview, but even this would not give further meaning to the story told.

On the other hand, the interview is a more natural situation, where the interviewee can feel more comfortable thanks to the ability of the interviewer to face or analyze the most sensitive issues.

There are different types of interviews that can be done based on how they are conducted, the techniques used and what we want to know.

With the simple interview there is a conversation with the interviewee about those issues proposed by the researcher, exploring the information that the interviewee finds more interesting.

A particular type of interview is the narrative one. It does not only reveal the different meanings that a person uses in order to make sense of the situations, but it also allows to access to the same situations.

It gives the possibility to observe through the eyes of the person.[55]

It can be said that the narrative interview is a tool used to reveal the personal experience, which contains both the possibility to see situations through the observer and to understand its meanings through listening.

The narrative interview is characterized by an active role of the interviewer, by the duration of the interaction and by the definition of the material format. The interviewer, being active in his role, chooses when and how to enter the narrative process.

He can participate, support, focus on and expand the story. In this type of interview, he is not neutral, instead he contributes controlling his own participation without ever influencing the content.[56]

---

[55] Denzin, NK & Lincoln, YS. (1994). "Introduction: Entering the field of qualitative research." In NK Denzin and YS Lincoln (Eds.) Handbook of Qualitative Research (pp. 1-17). Thousand Oaks: Sage Publications.
[56] Boje 1991, Gabriel 2000; Lieblich, Tuval-

The narrative interview lasts longer than other interviews. It can take from half a day to two or three days, this allows the interviewee to remember, dig deep, repeat sometimes the things already said, modify the story and expand his point of view. The interviewer asks the interviewee to tell him the experiences that the interviewee thinks are the most important in reference to the object of research. Stories will have to respect some rules such as the definition of the situation, the characters and the solutions.[57]

Mashiach, Zilber 1998. Gabriel, Y. (1998). "The use of stories." In G. Symon and C. Cassell (Eds.), "Qualitative methods and analysis in organizational research: A practical guide". 135-160. Thousand Oaks, CA: Sage.

[57] Propp, V., Morfologijaskazki, Leningrad, Academia, 1928, trad. it. Morfologia della fiaba, Torino, Einaudi, 1966. Greimas, A. J., Dusens II, Paris, Seuil, 1983, trad. italiana. Del senso 2, Milano, Bompiani, 1984.

## 3.2 *The interpretation of the narrative interview*

The goal of the narrative analysis on human life is interpretation and experience. Subjectivity is important in the autobiographical narrative process.

A search for meaning through interpretation. It is the opposite of the scientific experiment methods, which purpose is to discover laws.[58]

The interpretation concerns the meaning and the validity. However, often the meaning and the validity of the autobiographical narrative are not the same for the narrator and for the person who hears his story.

Important thing to do in the interpretation is to verify the story and explain its meaning.

The relationship between narrator and interviewer can influence the quality of the

---

[58] Josselson R., Lieblich A., "The narrative study of lives", Vol 3. Interpreting experience, Thousand Oaks, CA Sage,1995.

story. What is important is that there should be no tension between the two.

In the autobiographical interview the interviewee becomes the narrator of the story, while the interviewer guides and facilitates the process.

The two cooperate with each other in order to create a story that can satisfy the narrator.

Even though the autobiographical interview can be seen from a scientific point of view, it must be conducted as an artistic activity.[59]

Know and understand, how the narrative process is used in an interview can be as important as the questions chosen by the interviewer.[60]

In the autobiographical interview there are very few questions that must have a precise answer, since the goal is to give the interviewee the possibility to work on what happened on his own, to remember what he felt in those circumstances and maybe also how he feels years later.

---

[59] Atkinson R. 2006, "L'intervista narrativa", Raffello Cortina Editore.

[60] Holstein, Gubrium, The Active Interview, A sage University paper. 1995.

The same autobiographical story will never be observed in the same way by two researchers, since the narrative information can be analyzed in different ways, depending on the goal of the researcher

Even if there are instructions on how to conduct the interview, two people will never conduct the autobiographical interview in the same way. However, its transcript and interpretation, will only be one and specific, based on a selection of different criteria and choices.

The narrative interview is the result of a very personal relationship. The analysis of the autobiographical story is subjective and dependent on the quality and intensity of the personal exchange and on the theory that could be applied to the content of the story.

Between the narrator and interviewer, a creative reaction develops, which influences the story and how the story is told. The stronger and friendlier the relationship between the two is, the more elaborate the story gets.

Every story written by a different interviewer, will always show a different point of view, without ever changing the story itself.[61]

When telling a story, the person does not only say everything that has happened in his life.[62]

Telling a story means telling it from a certain point of view with an interpretive approach. Since the process is subjective, there are no formal procedure that can determine the validity of the story. However, there is an important standard indicator that can be used: the internal coherence.

How the personal story is told shows how the person sees the past, the present and the foreseeable future.[63]

What is said in a part of the story should not contradict what has already been said. Life is not coherent, so people will react in different ways, but the narration and the

---

[61] Frank, 1980; Runyan, 1982, "Handbook of review research", ed Sage Publication, 2001.

[62] Riessman, C.K. 1993. "Narrative Analysis". Qualitative Research Methods, Series, No. 30. Newbury Park, CA: Sage.

[63] Coheler B.J. Adversity, "Resilience, and the Study of Lives", University of Chicago, 1982

actions of the person should have an internal coherence.

The internal coherence is an important quality indicator, that can be used by both the interviewer and interviewee by comparing, if different, the initial comments and the following ones.[64]

The narration must be organic, copied into a text that must be clear for those who tell it, write it and read it.

Meaning can be given to life by connecting the events and from the story will emerge this directionality.[65]

About the external coherence, a correlation between what the person says, knows or thinks to know on the person who tells the story, is not always a good criterion, because we are not looking for the truth, but for the experience or the point of view of the narrator.

The narrative approach gives importance to the internal coherence as experienced by

---

[64] McCracken G., "The Long Interview, A Sage University" paper, 1988.
[65] Gergen, Kenneth J.; Gulerce, Aydan; Lock, Andrew; Misra, Girishwar "Psychological science in cultural context", American Psychologist, Vol. 51(5), May 1996, 496-503

the person and does not take into consideration the criteria of truth or external validity.

## 3.3 The place where stories are more powerful: the hospital.

The place of the interview is important when interviewing people with psoriasis. For a person that has had different hospitalization in his life, the hospital is surely a very particular place.

Patients enters a new social order, where they have to communicate with doctors and nurses, undergo medical examinations and tests, be cooperative and available for all the medical examinations that will be decided for them, for the medical protocol that the dermatologist will choose for them.[66]

The consequence is a psychological impact that can have defense reactions such as: anxiety, aggressiveness, regression, depression, isolation.

---

[66] Gammon, "The psychological impact of isolation", 1998.

All these defense reactions take part in the process of adaptation to reality.

Often, in the hospital does not matter how many people come to visit, to keep you company and to give you their support: there is a distance between those who are healthy and the patients, some sort of almost infinite space.

Moreover, in the life of a person with psoriasis, this can easily happen several times due to the different hospitalizations.

The physical environment of the hospital causes anxiety, frustration and depression. This happens for different reasons: being away from family, having to give up old habits, hospital organization, noises, limited space and having no privacy.

From the moment patients walks into a hospital they are already anxious because of the disease, and full of concerns, they also have to face different situations such as; wearing a pajama, so they have to give up their clothes, their symbols of personal identity, and meeting other sick people in their room.

Anxiety is very common since it can be caused by any aspect and stage of hospitalization.

Anxiety can cause physiological changes such as sleep disorder, high levels of excitability and irritability.

Aggressiveness can be caused by anxiety, fear of diagnosis and therapies, but mostly by the feeling that one's needs are not understood and satisfied.

Regression means a return to an earlier stage of life, followed by specific behaviors such as passive attitude and the need to be in someone else's care.

We have to remember that psoriasis is a chronic disease and requires multiple hospitalizations and this can cause the patient to lose hope in the therapeutic procedure and in the idea of healing.

The hospital becomes a nurturing place, since it creates a physical and mental space that separates the patient from the rest of the world: the patient is so nurtured and cured.

However, in a study conducted in an inpatient facility of the I.D.I. (Istituto Dermopatico dell'Immacolata in Rome), patients with psoriasis did not show aggressiveness and were cooperative[67]

---

[67] After giving patients a test of self-evaluation and

Patients with psoriasis have the tendency to avoid-deny feelings and conflicts. They do not show enough emotional intensity to the story they told. The consequence is unsociability, a psychological trait due to anxiety caused by the fear of being judged by others.

The 80% of patients said that psoriasis got better in response to a hospitalization after a stressful event.

So, the hospitalization plays a significant role in reducing emotional stress, but becomes inadequate if at the end of it the event has not lost its impact.

---

sense of Self, the result is that 63% of them see their life as stressful, 37% see their life as peaceful and 95% of the patients were ashamed and uncomfortable around others.

---

# Chapter IV: In the deep sea

## *4.1 Looking in the mirror*

Since I have this disease, I have decided to deepen my knowledge of the problems and complications that it entails.

Understand the difficulties of everyday life that every sick person encounters and has to face.

Psoriasis requires countless hospitalizations.

It causes painful and burning skin.

In addition, people with psoriasis cannot wear what they want, have to take medicines their entire life, avoid hands when greeting someone, are looked at as if they were monsters or contagious people, are avoided on purpose and have to face pitiful or disgusted looks.

Psoriasis is not a deadly disease, but it cannot be cured. In more severe cases, when living home, people are stigmatized.

It is a physical disease that causes a psychological discomfort that people who do not have it cannot understand.

Psoriasis leaves scars that are not only physical, but also psychological and social.

To better understand this disease, how sick people live, the difficulties of everyday life, I did not just study books and handbooks, but I also interviewed hospitalized patients.

It took me two years to interview them:

I started as a psychology student with psoriasis and then continued as a psychologist.

My main goal has been to try to understand what everyone hides inside themselves, the difficulties faced in everyday life and know which are the critical moments to overcome and why.

The myth of Narcissus shows how important and how dangerous looking at our own reflection can be.

As soon as Narcissus saw, for the first time in his life his reflection, he fell madly in love with the boy he was looking at, without realizing it was him.

Only after a while he understood that that was his reflection, but unlike the young man, when people with psoriasis look in the mirror, they never see beauty.

Other people's reactions, especially if the body part affected by the disease is visible, forces many people to isolate themselves; pain, itch and treatment duration can only make the quality of life worse.

This causes low self-esteem, changes in interpersonal relationships and countless limitations in work, cultural and social activities.

The stories told by the patients interviewed during these years of work, clearly show that people with psoriasis will never see themselves as beautiful.

Many were the interviews, but each one of them was meaningful and with a distinctive content.

Since it was impossible to write them all down here, I will only mention a few of them, that can successfully convey the life, pain and difficulties of the people interviewed.

Caterina[68] is a young woman, skinny and with a sad smile.

Several times I saw her cry while she was talking to someone.

At first, she did not want to be interviewed, then she changed her mind, saying that she needed to talk to someone who could understand her pain.

In the interview she explains in a simple and effective way how a person with psoriasis feels from a psychological point of view. The person needs to avoid looks from others, because only those who know the disease can really understand.

Caterina, however, although she has had the disease for many years, has not yet accepted it.

… Lately I am not okay with my body and myself, I feel psoriasis inside my body too, I am not okay.

I keep asking myself why me? Why do I have this disease? Was it unavoidable?

---

[68] The names of the people interviewed have been changed in order to protect their privacy. Caterina is a 26 years old married woman, housewife, interviewed by me when I was a patient.

I want it gone, I also thought about going to Lourdes, to use the holy water to heal… Only those who have this disease can understand you, who doesn't have it can see the skin inflammation, the burning sensation, imagine the pain, but cannot understand you. You must have it to understand.

Now I feel comfortable knowing that you have it and that you can understand me, but if I talk to someone who doesn't have it, it is like talking to a wall. They look at you and say that they understand, but in the end… they can't!

…There are days when I cannot put on makeup. My face is red, with patches, if I look at myself in the mirror I look like a clown. Instead of making it better, I make it worse.

When it is really bad, I don't feel comfortable, I don't want to be with other people, I avoid contact with others, I lock myself inside the house …

… My life has changed a lot since I got the disease, in sexual life, in everyday life, in the life with the people I hang out with. Psoriasis changes you, it changed me a lot.

I am trying to learn to live with it, but it is hard because it is impossible to live with something that hurts…

The disease causes insecurities in people. They do not feel good about themselves, because an important thing such as beauty, completely disappears.

Therefore, people with this disease feel the need to hide from the looks of strangers and sometimes also from the looks of loved ones.

The emotions and feelings of the person with psoriasis are damaged and become very fragile. Even the slightest problem or accident is often faced with great difficulty.

Giulia[69] is a middle-aged woman, a bit overweight due to her eating habits. In fact, she eats in order to reduce the anxiety caused by the disease.

At first, she had a friendly smile, but as the

---

[69] A woman of 51 years old, housewife, interviewed by me when I became a psychologist

interview went on that smile disappeared, replaced by tears and painful memories. Giulia said that since the disease she no longer had felt like the woman she was before.


… At the beginning when I was with my husband I always tried to turn off the lights. Even now, when we are intimate, I turn off the lights because I don't want him to see me.

With these "things" on my body, I am not like those beautiful women, I feel inferior… I neglect myself, because even if I put on makeup this disease is always with me…

I feel useless, I do not feel like a woman anymore…

I have to hide, if I go to the store and pick up the bread with these hands, I feel watched.

I feel bad and then I cannot control myself. Once I almost became like a homeless person, I didn't even shower anymore… I am very cheerful, before the disease, I was happy.

My children told me to go to the beach, maybe even topless and I always said that what I need is a rope and an anchor, not a thong because I am fat.

Now that I have these things, I'd rather not see anyone, I'd rather stay alone. My phone is always off too.

I feel better if I don't look at myself in the mirror, I feel better if I am alone.

If I talk with someone, I always feel watched.

Even my relatives don't know what I have, because they think it is contagious, so I tell them that it is an allergic reaction.

I feel sick inside, animals are doing better than me, I try to stay alone to cry. I once went to the hairdresser and the boy asked me if these things were contagious. I never went back there.

I felt like a leper, I felt sick and different. When I get out of here, I don't go to the grocery store, this must disappear first…


I talked about the beauty that influences self-esteem, this happens not only with women, but also with men. The disease forces them to change their routine, how they act and who they are. Luigi talks about it.[70]

I have this disease that is something that will never disappear, I live with this disease, I can handle it even if it causes a lot of problems.
Often, when I took the bus people distanced themselves from me. Often, at work I noticed that when I greet someone and try to shake their hand, they either avoid it or give me a pat on the shoulder. I am sure that who shook my hand then washed it immediately after. Even at the beach, in the water children distance themselves from me. When I had more scabs I didn't go to the beach, I stayed at home and cook, while my wife and children went there.

In the summertime I have to walk with long pants and closed shirts.

It is not normal during the summer, but unfortunately, I have to.

I get nervous when I think about it, but I would like to go to a dance school, but I cannot, because I would have to show my

---

[70] A57 years old man, steel fixer, interviewed by me when I became a psychologist.

hands.

If I think about it, I remember that I have never had a pimple in my life and then at twenty-five years old with this disease I suddenly felt ugly.

Not to mention with girls. I used to think see what happens, it is bad, really bad. Even today when I am at my house, I feel embarrassed when I am with my wife. In bed I remove the scabs that fall. Sometimes I use the vacuum and clean the entire house because I don't want to bother anyone. Many times, I say to myself: look what I have to do, what I have become.

… when I was young, I was obsessed with manicure. Now I cannot do it anymore and I tell myself that I am not the person I used to be.

My children get manicures, go to the barbershop, they look nice.

I remember that when I was their age, I used to do it too and I would like to do it again…

This disease, in severe cases, causes social exclusion. The person who has it feels forced to stay at home for some time, with the consequent work difficulties.

Here is what Eugenio thinks.[71]

We met while we were in line for hospital check-in. We were still wearing our clothes. Later, even though we were in different rooms, we got to know each other in the hospital aisles. Knowing about my research he was the first to volunteer, because he wanted to tell me his story, tell me as much as possible.

We understood each other. We looked like friends in the same battle, united against the enemy.


.... The problem is how you look, on my uniform the scales are more visible. When I talk to someone, the person keeps looking at my shoulder and not my face, ignores me and I feel awkward.

For work reasons I have to keep my hair short and when I have these red patches, I only feel comfortable around people who know about my disease, like my coworkers for example. Instead, if I meet someone that doesn't know about it, that person makes a

---

[71] A 37 years old man, soldier, interviewed by when I was a patient.

weird face, disgusted and I get nervous. There are many two-faced people.

When they are with you, they act like nothing is wrong, because it is convenient for them and they get close to you, but then they talk behind your back, saying that you don't wash yourself and that you have dandruff.

Once, a colleague discriminated me for what I had on my skin. He asked me what I had, maybe it was scabies, he told me with disdain!

I ignored it, because I knew it was no big deal, but it bothered me, it made me feel awful, different from other people. In the summertime I always feel watched. One time, I was at the gym, I had short hair because my skin needed to heal. A lot of them stared at me, avoided me and whispered among them.

While I was running on the treadmill, two women kept talking to each other while looking at me, making jokes. I couldn't hear what they were saying, but by the gestures and movement I understood that they were watching what I had on my head. I was upset, but I ignored them and moved on. I would like to jump in the waters of

Lourdes to heal. I undergo all the new medical treatments, but at the end nothing works for one reason or the other.

If I am not nervous or anxious, I do not let it bother me, but when I am, I scratch myself until I bleed. I cannot help myself. I have an advantage, because I have psoriasis where nobody can see it.

There are people who have it all over their body.

I think about the day they will go to the beach and take their clothes off, everyone on the beach will look at them ...

When the patches are on visible parts of the body, psoriasis alone or combined with the Psoriatic arthritis[72] has forced many people to leave their job sometimes momentarily, sometimes permanently.

---

[72] Is a long-terminflammatory arthritisthat occurs in people affected by psoriasis, it affects the joints. It occurs in about 5-30% of people affected by psoriasis. In Italy there are about 12.000-60.000 patients who have psoriatic arthritis.

There have been cases of sick people who felt forced to change the job they loved for a rebound one. This is the case of Antonio.[73] He quit his job. The disease took away from him the satisfaction to show his creativity through a job he loved. It forced him to live a life that he considers insignificant.


... after the onset of the disease, for a while I had anxiety, I felt inferior, I found it hard to be around people, I avoided shaking hands, I tried not to take my clothes off when I was at the beach.

I tried to avoid these situations because I was ashamed.

I felt watched because of my appearance, I isolated myself. No one isolated me, it was me, I was ashamed.

The disease changed my life, then I learned to live with it.

I feel pretty bummed when I have aches and I cannot walk properly.

---

[73] A 29 years old man, worker, interviewed by me when I was a patient.

I remember that when the disease started to appear on my skin I was a hairdresser, now I am a workman.

I couldn't pursue that career anymore because psoriasis appeared on my hands. A hairdresser with hands like this cannot work. They didn't fire me, I quit.

If it were not for this disease, I would have continued to be a hairdresser, because it is a creative and innovative career. But psoriasis forced me to change job.

Where I work now, I am just a number that goes to the factory and even if I don't go nothing changes, because someone else will go in my place.

I am just number.

Before if I made a good haircut, it was rewarding, now I cannot do it anymore. Now I try to be creative when I play music, because I like to play the piano.

But when the pain gets worst, I cannot even play that, it is depressing.

Now I cannot keep in touch with people like I used to. I avoid them because I don't want them to see me, also because they ask questions. I don't want to talk about it, I just want to forget about it.

A few weeks ago, I was in the changing room with a colleague that I have known by sight. To be honest, I don't like him. He looked at my hands and asked me what was wrong with them and I told him to go to…. hell. I told him to mind his own business. Someone who talks to me for the first time, cannot ask me anything.

When people have psoriasis, they are isolated, avoided by society and at work. Makes the ill person feel excluded from any social contact. This is the sad story of Filippo.[74]

This happens because there are still too many prejudices about this disease.

The form of the disease of Filippo was so severe that he could not get out of bed. He had a severe form of psoriasis all over his body. He could not get up, because every time he moved he felt excruciating pain.

Seven years ago, I had an acute episode of psoriasis. It started from the scalp and

[74] A 34 years old man, scrub nurse, interviewed by me when I became a psychologist.

face, then it covered the entire body. I let my beard grow like that of Moses. I used that beard to hide. I didn't leave the house for about twenty days.

I was a living scab. The dry skin cracked and bled, it was a complete metamorphosis. My lifestyle has changed in the last few years.

At first, I was in pain and cried. I went to a bar once and the barista gave me a disposable cup telling me that he couldn't give me the cup because he didn't know if I was contagious or not.

I went to the beach too, always with psoriasis all over my body, I got into the water and a mother immediately called her children to get them away from me.

Even though now I have learned to live with this disease, I still have not accepted it and I never will. One time I felt terrible and not for the aches and the pain caused by the disease, but for what a person told me at the hospital where I work.

I worked in an operating room, I had psoriasis on my hands and always used gloves, but a doctor told me that I could not stay there, because I could have contaminated the room.

At that moment I felt awful, I still remember her words: "and they have the courage to work in an operating room. With those hands he should work in an emergency room. I would not let him touch me if he were my boyfriend or my partner".

She started by talking about something related to work, and then she insulted me. That was bad. It would have been better if someone had given me a gun and told me to kill myself than hear something like that… today being thirty-four years old and lie in bed like this, without even be able to move or go to the bathroom is bad for my mental health.

The worsening of the disease or its appearance on specific parts of the body forces those affected to isolate themselves from society. This is what happened to Gennaro.[75]

---

[75] A 60 years old man, pizza maker, interviewed by me when I was a patient.

At first glance Gennaro looked like a tired man, weakened by the difficulties of life. But during the interview he revealed that he still had hopes of going back to his normal life.


… Is annoying when people stare at your hands and don't understand that it is not contagious.
I work as a pizza maker, so when I work you can see my hands. It bothers me when people look at me and make me feel like… I cannot describe it… it is really uncomfortable.
…when I work, I show my arms and hands, but how can I do it now that I am like this? At the moment, I have decided to take a break from work. How can I put these hands on a workbench? Personally, I didn't feel like working anymore.

This hospitalization will help me go back to work.
I have never been sick. I only had this disease, and the problem is only mine.

So, when people have psoriasis they are stigmatized, avoided by healthy people, isolated.

In some cases, people who do not have the disease avoid those who have it, while in other cases people with the disease isolate themselves. Listening to the story of Lino[76] we can understand the difficulties of everyday life. The pain that this isolation causes.

Lino is a short man, reserved, he seemed to be afraid of being heard. He is a man that would like to live his life peacefully, but unfortunately, he notices when people look at him and he feels uncomfortable.

During these years with the disease, I have become shyer, especially because of my hands. If I had to go to the store, or to the tobacco shop I used to hide my hands. …my life has changed because psoriasis made me shyer.

Even doctors asked me what I had. Some of them even distanced themselves from me

---

[76] A 51 years old man, retired, interviewed by me when I became a psychologist.

because they didn't know if it was contagious or not.

It didn't happen often, but it happened. I felt so angry because these things hurt. Anger just anger because the person in front of me didn't understand. This is just a disease.

Sometimes people distanced themselves from me, sometimes I had to hide my hands behind my back, because I didn't want people to see them.

This happened in the train, in the middle of the street, while talking to someone I didn't know... The disease bothers me, because it is on my hands, if my hands were clean, I wouldn't care so much about it.

At a wedding once, I felt so embarrassed. A lot of people didn't understand, they kept staring at me and I couldn't eat in peace. I couldn't eat, they looked at me strangely.

I felt ... I don't know, embarrassed, obviously.

During these years I have gone to the beach because my youngest daughter wanted to go. I went with her, but with my shirt on. I didn't take it off because I was full of patches, but I wanted to go into the water, so I went with my shirt on and then I let it dry on me.

There were too many people and I didn't feel like taking it off.

…what bothers me is my hands. If I didn't have it on my hands, I wouldn't think about it so much.

Fortuna[77] feels constantly watched too because of her disease. She feels like her life has been destroyed. She is in visible pain. Her face is not the face of a forty-year-old woman, she looks much older. In addition to preexisting problems, she has the disease too.

…I feel sick. I feel my skin burning, I feel something inside me. My life is over, I feel sick. Even the face. It will not disappear. I know that this disease gets better, but it never goes away. My life has gotten worst. I feel like jumping out of a window or go into the kitchen and…

---

[77] A 40 years old woman, housewife, interviewed by me when I became a psychologist.

Even though my life was already bad ten years ago, with this disease has gotten worse.
I have a lot of family problems and now I have another problem. Strangers judge you. I remember that on the bus people kept staring at me and it bothered me. I hid my hands. They looked at me strangely and I told them that it was not contagious. When I am alone, I hardly ever leave the house. I am scared. Sometimes I am scared of holding my three-moth-old nephew. I know that it is not contagious, but I cannot help it. When I have psoriasis, I lock myself in the house and never leave it...

When the disease can be easily hidden, people do not seem to worry about it too much. Roberto[78] talks about it.

Roberto says that his disease has never stopped him, because he could easily cover it with his hat. However, in the hospital he made it clear that it makes him

---

[78] A 68 years old man, retired, interviewed by me when I became a psychologist

uncomfortable. In fact, he went to the emergency room with his pajamas and a winter hat, even though it was really hot outside.

Actually, his strange way of hiding it drew more attention to it.


… Luckily, the disease has not really changed my life yet. Not even during this last year.

My disease is not noticeable. It would bother me more if it were, because until a month ago I was on television, since I am also a television journalist. It would bother me more if it became more visible and I could not go on television…

No one has ever noticed that I have it, because it was located on the body and the legs. It never appeared on the hands or the face. I had and have it on the scalp, but I wear a hat.

It bothers me when the scales fall off.

At night I apply the cream and go to sleep.

I worry that the cleaning lady may find it dirty, so I clean up before she comes … I don't worry too much about the disease. Even though for the last two or three weeks my legs have been very painful, I know it is not lethal …


These interviews clearly show how strong and sometimes dramatic the impact on the patient's quality of life can be.

A patient who must also face physical and psychological consequences.

The body is in a lot of pain and when the disease is noticeable, the patient could also have to face social discrimination, which can have consequences on the person's mental health.

## 4.2 Know oneself

All the stories told to both the psychologist and the patient show that almost every interviewee wants to hide the disease.

If it is not noticeable, like on the hands or the face, they try to hide it and try not to think about it too much. This also happens when it is mild.

On the other hand, people who have a visible disease, do not leave the house in order to hide it, because they feel ashamed. They are ashamed of themselves and of how they look.

Hiding is possible until the opportunity of going to the beach arises. They cannot hide anything there. They all must show themselves as they are.

In that moment they all have to face difficulties and problems.

The sea is important, not only because it can relax, but also because sun exposure is good for the skin, even better if close to the sea[79]

Sunlight triggers the synthesis of the vitamin D within the body.

This vitamin regulates the absorption of calcium in our bone and helps fight osteoporosis. in addition, vitamin D is also important for the immune system.[80]

---

[79] Carlo Solaroli, head dermatologist at the Hospital Maggiore of Bologna, believes that the type A radiation is what is good for the skin. The type A radiation can go deeper into the skin and reach the dermis.

This is why the Dead Sea is known for its healing properties against psoriasis. Being 400 meters below sea level, the additional atmospheric layer, minimize the passage of type B radiation (which causes erythema, the redness of the skin) letting the Uva spread instead.

[80] Psoriasis is an autoimmune disease, a condition where the immune system does not attack a bacterial or viral infection, but causes an inflammatory process which damages an organ or a tissue.

Sunlight helps our body produce growth hormone, which is not only important for the growth of children, but also contributes to the health of bones, hair and skin in adults.

Moreover, the seawater, contains minerals such as sodium, sulfur and copper, which have positive effects on people with eczema and psoriasis.

The air too is rich in mineral salts which our organism assimilates through breathing. When the waves move, sodium chloride, magnesium, iodine and potassium particles are released.

Moreover, since the sea is an unknown and unpredictable place, has different meanings. The surface is visible, but it has depths that the human eye cannot see.

To swim we have to take off our clothes, reveal our body and the people affected by psoriasis also have to reveal their emotional insecurities.

In the sea there is the marine environment which represents the Other.

When we go into it, that infinite space becomes too tight.

The same thing happens on the beach and on the seashore where the other becomes too close.

The sea represents the here and now of the disease. Here we have to face problems that need to be solved, sudden and unexpected situations.

Our body is not used to listen to our needs, but becomes the source of the problem since the social environment marginalizes and despises the exterior appearance of the people affected.

The thick skin becomes an armor.

It protects us from emotional exchanges with the outside.

Since it no longer conforms to the common social beauty standards, it becomes the object of social stigmatization. Going to the sea means getting in touch with our own body, our inner self and personality.

Something that is already difficult for the person affected by psoriasis, becomes impossible due to the disease.

I will only transcribe some excerpts from the interviews, the most powerful.

I remember Gennaro[81], a short man, with white hair and dark skin. A man of few words at first, but he opened up to me twice. The first time when I was a patient and the second time after two years, when I became a psychologist.

The second time, at first he did not remember me, but then he recognized me and was very happy to see me. He asked me how my studies were going and he congratulated me for my achievements. When he was with me he did not hide his feelings and tears.

He saw psoriasis as a punishment, the worst thing that could happen to him.

The colorful language he used when talking about the disease hid his anger and pain.

A pain bottled up inside him without a way out.

His words are the kind of words that can make you feel powerless and in pain.

---

[81] A man, 63 years old, sanitation worker, interviewed by me the first time when I was a patient and the second time when I became a psychologist.

... It is a disease you have to live with, you have to live with it even if you hate it.

I hate it and I am ashamed when I am with my wife and children.

It bothers me.

It bothers me when my wife looks at me, even though she never said anything, I sometimes avoid her.

Physically I feel fine, but psoriasis makes me feel ashamed.

Even at the work if I have to take a shower I don't, I go home and shower there...

I feel sick, it hurts, I cannot stand it. I can't even look at myself in the mirror.

If I move my clothes the skin falls off, my wife has to sweep the floor and looks at me and tells me to be careful.

I feel clean inside, but I feel dirty outside.

I hate it. it is appearing on my hands too and when I am in front of other people I hide them ...

Not to mention the beach, I do not go there. it has been almost fifteen years since the last time I went to the beach.

During the summer, I sunbathe on the terrace.

Even though sunlight is good for you and I

know that, I don't go to the beach, I cannot, I would rather go on the terrace of my house.

I have eight grandchildren, so I would like to go to the beach... here he stopped telling the story, because he started to cry.

After two years he started talking about the sea again, he felt better about his psoriasis and finally went to the beach. However, he was not completely healed so he went alone, because he still felt ashamed in front of his nephews. He did not want them to see him as a monster.

...I have never been able to go to the beach. When I went there, I went alone. I didn't want people to see me, especially kids, they can get scared. Mothers might tell them to stay away from me.

I went to the beach, but I didn't let anyone see me, I didn't want to be seen. I went to the beach dressed, I was wearing my swimsuit, but always with the t-shirt on, I never took it off. I went into the water with my shirt on.

It is not easy to go to the beach with eight grandchildren and not get undressed. They make questions, they asked me several times to go into the water and play with them and I always make excuses saying that I have to work or something.

My wife makes excuses too and my grandchildren always complain that I never go with them and that I don't love them. It is frustrating, it makes you feel bad about yourself.

I have eight grandchildren and I cannot go to the beach with them.

This is awful ...


Isolate themselves from other, from their relatives and friend, in order to go to the beach and benefit from the therapeutic properties of the sea, is something that people with this disease have always done. Peppe[82] is a old man who has had psoriasis for over fifty-one years, so listening to his story was like walking into a library where the books talk about centuries of history and culture.

An old and though man, but with a very sweet and sad story.

---

[82] A 71 years old man, interviewed by me as a psychologist.

Listening to him felt like taking a step back in time. There are many people who have had this disease for years, but listening to a person that has had it for fifty years allows access to a wide range of emotions.

... It was harder when I was young, because it appeared on my hands. Luckily it didn't appear on my hands again. When it happened I always tried to hide it, but it was difficult at work.

Thankfully, I have never had it on my face, but I could not go to the beach with my friends. When I could, I went alone, I always went on the rocks because I didn't want to be seen. I didn't want my friends or anyone else to see me.

I isolated myself because I felt different and excluded. I remember that when I was hospitalized, the first time, I was young and I cried, I cried every night.

... This disease, when it is on the face, the hands and therefore can be seen, causes problems and discomfort, but if it is located where it cannot be seen it causes less problems. The disease is not as it was fifty years ago, it is better now. In addition, people today, both friends and strangers are less wary.

Years ago people were more uninformed, today life has changed, people know more, rarely there is someone who doesn't know about psoriasis.

This disease can arise at any age. Obviously, the negative effect is worst on young people.

This happened to Elisa[83] who didn't go to the beach behind the rocks like Peppe did. She ran away from her city in order to benefit from the therapeutic properties of the sea. She went as far as possible, where no one knew her.

I am ashamed of this, in fact, many of my friends know that I am hospitalized, but they don't know why. I didn't tell them, I don't have the courage. I know they wouldn't tell me anything, but I cannot accept it, so I cannot let other people accept it...

People are ignorant, many people look at you and think that you are contagious and so you isolate yourself, because that is what happened.

---

[83] A 23 years old woman, process server, interviewed by me as a psychologist.

This was my first summer with psoriasis. I went to Calabria, because no one knows me there, I could never go to the beach here in Naples.

Anyway, every time I arrived at the beach it was so hard, a lifeguard gave me courage, he is an old man in his seventies.

He gave me the strength, he asked me what it was, he encouraged me to sunbathe, saying that there were more severely affected individuals and that mine was a mild form of psoriasis.

Then I started to notice some improvements, because with the sun it disappeared. Only the legs and sides were still affected. I was always sunbathing, in fact my skin became much darker, when I came back to Naples everyone asked me where I had been, because my skin was so much darker. From noon until six in the evening I sunbathed on an inflatable lounger tied to a buoy in the middle of the sea.

... if I only think about wearing a skirt and show these legs I feel sick. I will never wear a skirt, for sure... in the wintertime, if a wear shorts I always wear very thick stockings too, so people cannot see my legs, this is how I hide the disease. I just hide it, nothing more.

... I still have a complex, that is my complex... if other people see me, it's disgusting.

I never tell people that I am affected by this disease, maybe because I am ashamed, maybe they judge me, look at me, I don't know.


Even though the sea is important for the healing process, it does not mean that being always by the sea makes people immune to the disease. As in the case of Sergio[84], a fisherman.

A short and burly man, with the wrinkles of a person who has spent his life in the sun. He was a roommate, who always wanted to talk, ask for explanations and comfort those who were younger than him.

A simple man, spontaneous, sincere.

I still remember the bottle of wine he hid into his locker and that he used to make a

---

[84] A 56 years old man, fisherman, interviewed by me when I was a patient.

toast to his happiness, his rebirth, after his recovery.

The sea represents for him life and hope for a complete recovery. His tears show his dream to be clean again and without those "tracchie" (this is how he calls psoriasis).


... During the summer it disappeared from the head, but in January it appeared in other places too. It was all over my body, on the hands, the feet. I can even feel it inside my stomach, it affected my stomach. I used to come home and not eat, whenever I saw food I felt sick. I lost almost ten kilos in two months.

I used to leave the house at four in the morning and come back home at fourteen and not eat, I never ate.

Tomorrow I'll be out, I am so happy, I am finally clean, I am going home clean. I will never wear my hat again. Everyone must know that I have recovered.

I am never going to wear my hat again. Everyone has to see me without hat and gloves. I have to shake hands and... hell! eh eh eh.

Now I don't have to think about my hands. With all those scabs on my hands I couldn't do anything.

My wife had to feed me, wash me, help me get dressed. Tomorrow when the doctor tells me that I can go, I will leave. I won't call my son to come pick me up, I have to surprise them at home, they have to see me come back home clean.

But first, if the doctor says I can drink, I have to stop by the bar with my friends.

But tomorrow, even if the doctor says I can't, I will have a drink with my friends anyway.

I feel revealed, the hospitalization was worth it, I was a monster, a monster and... now I am a newborn.

I wish it'd disappear, but it will reappear. I pray god that it won't reappear...let the wind take it! I wish the wind, the sea will take it away forever...

The sea has several psychological meanings. It is dynamic and never the same.

It flows, transforms. It is deep, therapeutic. Brings energies that can heal.

It has no beginning and no end. It is the beginning of life and death.[85]

The sea has several meanings for people with psoriasis too; it represents a cure for the disease, thanks to its beneficial and healing effects, but it also represents social exclusion and marginalization which causes the worsening of the disease.

In fact, in a person affected by psoriasis, the emotions, conflicts, anger, are repressed and therefore the recovery seems impossible to the patient who feels even worst.

---

[85] In the Bible (Genesis), in the Koran, in the Hindu mythology, water is the place where all living creatures are born. Like Thales of Miletus said in the VII century b. C., the liquid element is everywhere. The sea does not only represent life, it also represent mystery and fear of death. Homer in the Odyssey talks about people who die in the sea after being enchanted by the siren's songs.
With the great flood, God floods the earth with sea water and humans die.

## 4.3 Co-Exist with psoriasis

The disease affects the life of the people who suffer from it. It affects even the simplest activities, such as eating or get dressed, or simply get a coffee with friends. But it can also affect a person's state of mind and social status.

Psoriasis can get better with age when the person affected learns to live with the disease.

It is a chronic disease. It tends to go through cycles, so the people affected have to live with the disease.

Psoriasis affects the self-esteem and the individual can become more fragile and change his or her relationship with society. Self-esteem is positive or negative attitude that people have towards themselves.[86]

---

[86] Rosenberg, M. (1965). "Society and the adolescent self-image". Princeton: Princeton University Press.

If people "love" themselves, it is positive, but if people do not love themselves it is "negative".[87]

People affected by psoriasis have three defense mechanisms; they hide their disease by covering themselves with hats, pants or long-sleeved shirts even during the summer. They hide the characteristics on which social stigma is based. They try to justify their disease[88], especially in social situations, when they seek the support of those who suffer from the same stigma.[89] Those who are affected by severe cases of psoriasis isolate themselves from the outside world, they do not leave their house for months.

---

[87] Blascovich, J., & Tomaia, J. (1993). "Measures of self-esteem." In P. R. Robinson & L.S. Wrightsman. "Measures of personality and social psychological attitudes". Ann Arbor: Institute for Social Research

[88] Describing it as a different disease, for example by saying that it is dandruff or a simple non-infectious allergy.

[89] Goffman Stigma. Stigma. "L'identità negata", translated by Roberto Gianmarco, collection "«Psicologia sociale e clinica della devianza», Giuffrè, 1983.

Narcissus's mother got rid of every reflecting surface in the house, and the same thing happens with those affected by psoriasis who always try not to look at themselves in the mirror and try to hide from others because they do not want to be judged.

The disease of a person affected by psoriasis becomes a social identity. It also categorizes the individual by putting him into a group with characteristics of stigma and rejection.[90]

The individual would thus be characterized by the disease and his social identity would be associated with his collocation in a system of social categories determined by the characteristics of the disease. So, in people affected by psoriasis the Self represents the result of a dialectic tension between what they feels inside and what is shown outside.

The Self of people with psoriasis is based on the judgements and signs of

---

[90] Michael Billig, Henri Tajfel. "Social categorization and similarity in intergroup behavior", 1972.

recognition or denial that other people give them.[91]

Therefore, the Self is a process where the individual and society are the protagonists. It is dialectical. Subjective factors and the social world act both as a representation of the other and as a system of relations.

People who had psoriasis in places that could easily be covered by clothes, hid the disease and did not even tell their friends, they only told their families. Some people did not even talk about it with their close relatives.

The patients interviewed chose to tell their story because they had the opportunity to talk to a person who was sick too.

---

[91] C.H. Coley, Yeung, King-To, and Martin, John Levi. "The Looking Glass Self: An Empirical Test and Elaboration."; Social Forces 81, no. 3 (2003): 843-879.

According to Coley the Self is a social construct which implies the interiorization of other meanings. People makes their own the behaviors that other people have towards them. This represents the looking-glass-self. Which means that we base our sense of self on how others see us, by using the attitude others use toward us.

They thought that the interviewer could understand the humiliating and stressful situations, that "healthy" people cannot understand.

Strangers, people who do not know about the disease, cannot understand how uncomfortable it is, but if they do know it, then they can understand the pain.

Therefore, people with psoriasis can only talk with people who are affected too, maybe this is the reason why they opened up to the patient-interviewer who was also hospitalized or with the psychologist who is an expert in the field.

The interviews show how important clothes such as hats and gloves are.

These items hide the disease when it appears on the hands or on the head.

Besides, even those who have or had psoriasis in less visible places could not go to the beach, where people have to show their whole body.

They had to find isolated places and go without friends or loved ones.

All the interviewees talked about the sea, even though they were never asked to talk about it.

In the second part, the people affected had the opportunity to talk to a psychologist, so they also talked about other problems.

Problems that they would rather tell a phycologist than a patient, because they believed that could be more useful. They talked about how uncomfortable they were, how hard their daily life was, how difficult it is when they have to show not only their body, but also their emotions; fear, shame.

Usually, people affected by psoriasis do not talk to relatives or friends that are not close. The disease does not "start" with the first spots, but when a diagnosis is made. [92]

Most patients see this disease as a condemnation that will force them to always take into consideration the disease when talking to others.

---

[92] How doctors tell their patients they are affected by psoriasis shows how a specific culture perceives the concept of vulnerability- disease and death. Since psoriasis is a non-fatal disease, doctors tell their patients without taking into consideration that even though it is not deadly, the disease causes lifelong problems. Not only dermatological problems, but also social and psychological ones.

This disease will influence their daily life, lifestyle, work and relationships forever. They will always fear the look of disgust and fear in the eyes of others, and they will always be afraid of being avoided.

People affected by psoriasis will always remember the past as a better time when they were not ill.

The present will become more and more difficult due to the fact that the disease is chronic and always reappears. People will lose hope, because they know that they will never heal completely.

It is when psoriasis affects parts of the body that cannot be hidden behind clothes that they feel the most uncomfortable.

All the information was gathered from the two types of interviews.

The interviewees were all willing to talk, but almost all patients, when talking to a psychologist, have also expressed their feelings.

They did not start the interview by talking about their daily life problems, this information only came out later on. Also, it is clear that the way people react to the disease is based on where the disease appeared and at what age.

People with psoriasis have problems at work and feel embarrassed. Moreover, due both to their appearance and the fact that they cannot move their hands, they also stopped working.

Psoriasis does not only affect work and relationships, but if it develops around the genital areas people cannot even have a normal sex life, for both physical and psychological reasons.

All the patient interviewed said that they immediately told everyone, relative, friends, colleagues, strangers, that they were not contagious.

When people asked them about their disease, they said it was caused by stress, without getting too much into details, because they did not know much about it either or because they did not want to talk about it.

The interviews and the observations made in the clinic and in the ward, show that people affected by psoriasis want to talk about their disease with people who know it or with those who are also affected. At the same time, they believe that talking with someone that does not know about it is useless.

In the clinic the majority of people observed try to talk to other patients while waiting. They talk until they have to be examined.

This is why I choose to interview those who were in the ward, because it is a quiet place and we had more time there.

In the ward there is no common area where people can talk.

In order to talk they have to meet in the hallway, in the hospital rooms or at the entrance of the building.

Many drew attention to the fact that there is no psychological support, no one explains the characteristics of the disease and tries to comfort them.

There should be self-help groups[93] where people can communicate and support each other, thus becoming a coping strategy.[94]

---

[93] The definition that WHO (world health organization) gave of Self-help is that it is a combination of all the measures taken by nonprofessional figures to promote, preserve and regain health. Health meant as complete physical, psychological and social wellbeing of a community. These groups are used by people that have the same problem and that can gather to support each other. Participants become part of a group, recover

The physical and biological problems due to psoriasis, in addition to the psychological ones, make it impossible for the person to look in the mirror. People are scared of their own reflection, but they are also afraid of being judged, stigmatized by others. Narcissus's myth, that I have mentioned many times, allows to understand the power of images, of the body and the role that people give them.

To Narcissus the reflected image symbolizes the interpersonal relationship that he avoids when he does not recognize the other, but the other is his reflection.

In people with psoriasis their reflection in the eyes of others becomes worse than what

---

their social responsibility and contribute to the wellbeing of the community. People with the same problems can share their own experiences, tell others how to face problems based on their own experiences. In these groups people both give and take emotional help and social support.

[94] Coping strategies define the adaptation process to a situation which is considered stressful by the person. The active coping strategies are attempts that people make in order to somehow control their pain. The attempt to act normal, despite the pain or the problem itself.

---

it really is, when followed by expressions of disgust or disdain.

# Bibliography

- Abeni D., Picardi A., Pasquini P., Melchi CF., Chern MM (2002) "Further evidence of the validity and reliability of the Skindex-29: an italian Study on 2.242 dermatological outpatients". Dermatology 204:43-9.

- Anderson RT, Rajagopalan R. (1997). "Development and validation of a quality of life instruments for cutaneous diseases". J Am Acad Fermato; 37: 41-50.

- Anzieu D.,1985, "L'io pelle", Roma, Borla, 1994.

- Atkinson R. (2006), "L'intervista narrativa", Raffaello Cortina Editore.

- Bichi R., 2002, "L'intervista biografica. Una proposta

metodologica". Milano. Vita e pensiero.

- Braathen LR, Botten G, Bjerkedal T. Psoriatics in Norway. Acta Derm Venereol 1989; 142 (Suppl): 9-12.

- Chren MM, Lasek RJ, Quinn LM et al. (1996) "Skindex, a quality-of-life measure for patients with skin disease: reliability, validity, and responsiveness". J Invest Dermatology; 107: 707-71313.

- Cicognani E. (2002), "Psicologia sociale e ricerca qualitativa", Carocci editor, Roma.

- Cotterill JA Cunliffe WJ. Suicide in dermatological patients. Br J Dermatology 1997; 137: 246-250.

- Dipboye R., Arvey R. Terpstra D., 1977, "Sex and physical attractiveness of raters and applicants as determinants of résumé evaluations", "Journal of Applied Psychology", 62, 288-294.

- Feingold A., (1992), Good-looking people are not we think, "Psychological Bullettin" 21, 304-341.

- Finlay AY, Coles EC. "The effect of severe psoriasis on the quality of life of 369 patients". Br J Dermatology 1995; 132: 236-244.

- Flick U. (1998). "An introduction to qualitative research". London. Sage

- Fortune DG, Richards HL, Main CJ et al. "What patients with psoriasis believe about their condition". J Am Acad Dermatology 1998; 39: 196-201.

- Freud A. (1936), "L'Io e i meccanismi di difesa". Florence. Martinelli, 1967.

- Freud S. (1922), "L'io e l'Es" in Opere, Vol. 9, Turino, Boringhieri, 1977, p. 488.

- Gaddini E. (1982), "Il Sé in psicoanalisi", Milan, Cortina.

- Ginzburg IH, Link Bg. (1993) "Psychosocial consequences of rejection and stigma feelings in psoriasis patient". Int J Dermatology; 32: 587-91.

- Glaser B.G. e Strauss A.L. (1967), "The discovery of Grounded

Theory: Strategies for Qualitative Research", Chicago, Aldine.

- Goffman E., "La vita quotidiana come rappresentazione", 1959. Italian translation. Bologna, Il Mulino, 1969.

- Goffman E., "Stigma", 1963, italian translation, Verona, Ombre corte, 2003.

- Kavli G, Forde OH, Arnesen E, et al. "Psoriasis: familial predisposition and environmental factors". Br Med J 1985: 291: 999-1000.

- LipowskiZj, "Psychosomatic medicine in the seventies: an overview". Am J Psychiatry 1977: 134: 233-234.

- Mantovani. "Manuale di Psicologia sociale", 2003.

- McHenry PM, Doherty VR. "Psoriasis: an audit of patients' views on the disease and its treatment". Br J Dermatology 1992 127: 13-7.

- Naldi L, Parazzini F, Brevi A, et al. "Family history, smoking habits, alcohol consumption and risk of psoriasis". Br J Dermatology 1992; 127:212-217.

- Ramsay B. O' Reagan M. "A survey of the social and psychological effects of psoriasis". 1988: 195-201.

- Rapp SR, Feldman SR. Exum ML et al. "Psoriasis causes as much disability as other major medical disease". J Am Acad Dermatology 1999; 41: 401-407.

- Rowatt W. C., Cunningham M. R., Druen P. B., 1999, Lying to get a date: The effect official physical attractiveness on the willingness to deceive prospective dating partners, "Journal of Social and Personal Relationships" 16, 209-223.

- Savin P. "Psychosocial aspect. In: Textbook of psoriasis" (Van de Kerkohf P. ed.). Oxford Blackwell Science 1999: 43 – 51.

- Smith J.A. (1995), "Semi-structured interviewing and qualitive analysis", in J.A. Smith R. Harrè e l.van Langenhove, rethinking Methods in Psychology, London Sage pp. 9-26.

- Strauss J. e Corbin (1990), "Basics of Qualitative Research. Grounded Theory Procedures and Techniques", Newbury Park, Sage.

- Strauss J. e Corbin A. (1994), "Grounded Theory Methodology. An Overview", in N.K. Denzin e Y.S. Lincoln (eds.), Handbook of Qualitative Research, Thousand Oaks, Sage, pp. 273-285.

- Strauss J. e Corbin A. (1998), "Grounded Theory Methodology. An Overview", in N.K. Denzin e Y.S. Lincoln (eds.), "Strategies of Qualitative Inquiring", Thousand Oaks, Sage, pp. 158-183.

- Van Dorssen IE, Boom BW, Hengeveld MW. "Experience of sexuality in patients with psoriasis and constitutional eczema". Ned Tijdschr Geneeskd 1992; 136: 2175-8.

- Waters J. (1985), Cosmetics and the job market. In J. Graham, A. Kligman (eds.), "The Psychology of cosmetics treatments", New York, Praeger.

- Winnicott, D. (1960). "The theory of the parent-child relationship"., Int. J. Psychoanal., 41:585–595.

- Wright V. Moll JMH. "Psoriatic arthritis". In: Wright V. Moll JMH editors. Seronegative polyarthritis. Amsterdam: North Holland Publishing, 1976: 169-233).

- Zani B. Cicognani E., "Psicologa delle salute", Società ed. il Mulino, Bologna, 2000.

# The author

Giovanni Salierno is a clinical psychologist and psychotherapist who works as a freelancer.

With a degree in: Economia e Commercio, then he got a degree in: Psicologia dei Processi Relazionali e di Sviluppo.

Then majored in: Psicologia Clinica e di Comunità at the University of Naples Federico II.

He also has a three years master degree in: Psicodiagnostica and specialization in Psicoterapia: Sistemico-Relazionale e Familiare.

He earned the title of: TangoTerapeuta.

Several were the hospitalizations, the treatments and medications over the years.

He met many doctors and many patients like him who had the same disease.

All this made him write this book, so that people like him, can find support and help.

Now he lives in Naples and works with different private associations.

He also organizes different emotional paths of psychophysical wellbeing through group works.

# Contacts

**Facebook page:**
Dottor Giovanni Salierno

**Facebook group:**
L'illusione di Eco ... l'inganno di Narciso

**Instagram:**
Dottor_Giovanni_Salierno

# Acknowledgments

...thanks to Professor
Caterina Arcidiacono

... special thanks ...to my mother
...she knows why

www.ingramcontent.com/pod-product-compliance
Lightning Source LLC
Chambersburg PA
CBHW021147260726
48656CB00025B/1610